WITHDRAWN

we can work it out

CONFLICT RESOLUTION FOR CHILDREN

BARBARA K. POLLAND, Ph.D.

Photographs by Craig DeRoy

Tricycle Press
Berkeley, California

This book is dedicated to David Hinds, an authentic optimist who knew how to encourage, how to inspire, and how to love. May his light continue to shine far beyond his too-short life.

ACKNOWLEDGMENTS

Sincere appreciation to Nicole Geiger of Tricycle Press, for encouraging me to write this book, and to Cybele Knowles, a tireless, excellent editor. Thank you to the following people for their meaningful friendship and their belief in me: Bonnie Karlin, Cheryl Smith, Mari Yoneda, Connie Tunick, Dianne Philibosian, Jeanne Axler, Sue Hanna, Bertl Maier, Betsy Reilly, Butch Schuman, Jeff Colby, the Ettenheims, Honey and George DeRoy, Don and Donna Dorsey, and Gene and Lee Kay. Much gratitude for seventeen years of caring and learning with my wonderful parents' group: Judy Flesh, Shirley Hulsey, Ronnie Lippin, and Caroline McWilliams. How thankful I am that my own dear parents and I 'worked it out'! Craig DeRoy made every photo shoot a positive experience. His sensitivity behind the camera lens was equally evident in his delightful interpersonal relationships with the fantastic children and adults who let us capture their images for this book. Last and never least, I'm so grateful for my children, Tamy and Mark, who are my very best teachers and blessings.

TRICYCLE PRESS
P.O. Box 7123
Berkeley, California 94707
www.tenspeed.com

Text and cover design by Toni Tajima
The text of this book was set in MetaPlus

Library of Congress Cataloging-in-Publication Data
Polland, Barbara Kay, 1939-
We can work it out: conflict resolution for children / Barbara K. Polland; photographs by Craig DeRoy.
    p. cm.
Summary: Text and photographs designed to create opportunities for children to talk about their experiences of conflict and the varieties of ways to resolve them.
    ISBN 1-58246-031-0 -- ISBN 1-58246-029-9 (pbk.)
    1. Conflict management--Juvenile literature. [1. Conflict management.] I. DeRoy, Craig, ill. II. Title.
HM1126.P67 2000
303.6'9--dc21
                                              00-023852

First printing, 2000
Printed in China
2 3 4 5 6 — 04 03 02 01

CONTENTS

WELCOME PARENTS AND TEACHERS

The goal of this book is to encourage conversations between adults and children about typical conflicts children encounter. The words and the photographs have been designed to create many opportunities for children to talk about problems and ways to resolve them.

In our roles as parents and teachers, one of our most important jobs is effectively socializing the children in our lives. We need to help them learn to determine right and wrong for themselves and act accordingly. Discipline is one of the best tools we have for guiding young people. However, discipline is often understood to mean simply punishment, when it needs to be so much more. The ultimate goal of discipline, after all, is self-discipline. If we want children to learn to resolve problems, then discipline needs to be something we do *with* them, not *to* them. When children remain dependent on adults to resolve all their issues, they are slow to develop the skills to solve problems on their own. But when they are authentically involved in problem-solving, they begin to acquire effective ways to cope.

When conflicts occur, it's important to avoid power struggles. Our age and size put us in the position of being able to easily overpower our children in physical and emotional ways. Forcing children into compliance doesn't teach them the problem-solving skills they need to learn. Likewise, punishment often prevents families from working on viable solutions, leaving everyone feeling upset. To find a guideline, we can ask ourselves if we are treating children in the way we hope that they will treat us and each other.

Most of us would be shocked if given an accurate accounting of the number of corrections and criticisms a child endures each day. Frequent criticism may increase children's feelings of inadequacy, frustration, failure, and anger. Instead, we need to tell children much more about what they're doing that is appropriate.

Of course, there are days when we will become tense and irritable over conflicts. Our challenge as adults is to keep those days to a minimum, remembering the fact that problems present teachable (not preachable) moments for learning. Children generally behave as we behave, mimicking our actions and our tone of voice. By acting constructively rather than aggressively, we model appropriate behavior.

The following three steps offer a framework to help stay focused on productive conflict resolution. This approach relies on the mutual respect of adults and children along with an attitude of determination to succeed.

1. Each person involved in a conflict needs to figure out what happened and how everyone feels about it. An accepting, safe emotional environment, free of ridicule, is basic to this approach. In the beginning many children blame others for everything that happens, but eventually they can learn to recognize and take responsibility for their role in creating problems.

2. Children and adults should list several possible solutions to the problem. Thinking of multiple solutions teaches children that there are many different ways to solve any problem. Together, adults and children should select the first solution to try.

3. Review the steps everyone took to solve the conflict. Once a problem has been resolved, most people are happy to forget about it. The review process reinforces the specific skills used to reach a successful conclusion to a conflict situation. Congratulate each other for contributions made to the problem-solving process. Success breeds success, and children who feel capable are likely to perpetuate positive resolution approaches. Keep in mind that when compliments are too predictable children tend to dismiss them, so we need a variety of ways to congratulate each other. This book offers fourteen examples for celebrating success.

The tools children learn from participating in the three steps can help them in conflict situations whether an adult is present or not. Please use this book as a way to encourage children to discuss conflicts in a calm and safe environment. Listen to their thoughts without judging them and let them know you appreciate their perspective. At the end of the book children are encouraged to send in any of their ideas for conflict resolution. Know that your ideas would also be appreciated!

LET'S BEGIN

Do you ever cry, yell, or fight because you feel really upset?

Do people ever get upset with you?

Everyone has problems getting along with others sometimes. How often does this happen to you?

This book is filled with pictures and questions about conflicts that happen a lot. As you read and talk about the things you see, you'll find good ways for people to help each other solve problems.

teasing

- Why do some people like to hurt other people's feelings?

- What is the meanest thing anyone ever said to you?

- Is it hard or easy to forget those words?

- What is the meanest thing you've ever said to someone?

kindness

■ What could you say that might get the teasers to stop?

■ Who could help you tell someone you're angry without sounding mean?

Give me five!

kindness

hitting

- Has anyone ever been so angry with you that they started pushing or hitting?

- Did that make you angry or scared? Did you want to push or hit them back?

- Is it hard or easy for you to stay in control of your fists?

controlling fists

- Why do adults tell children to use words, not fists?

- When is it okay to fight back?

- Can you think of two different ways to solve angry situations without physical fights?

- Make a list of things that are okay to hit, and things that are not okay to hit.

controlling

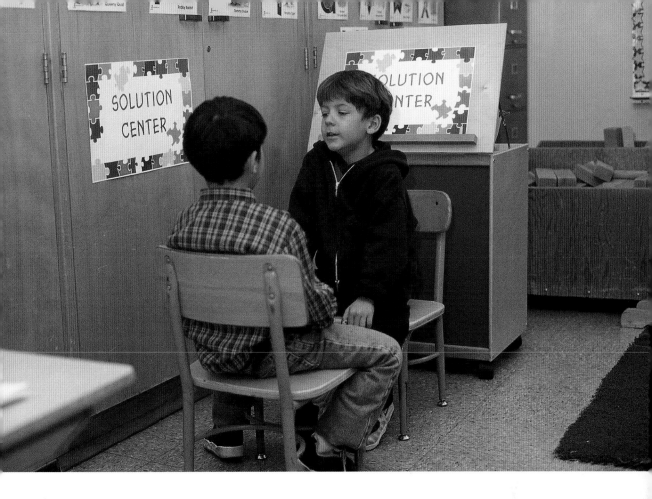

fists

Let's shake on it!

criticism

- Has anyone ever told you that they don't like something about you? What did they say?

- How did you feel about their words and about them?

- Should people always say what they don't like about each other?

compliments

- Can people learn from criticism?

- What is a really nice thing someone once said to you?

- Think of three people you could say nice things to. Be sure to tell those people what you like about them.

Let's be friends!

blaming

- When was the last time you were really mad at someone?

- Why is it so easy to blame others when things go wrong?

blaming

taking
responsibility

- Did you ever try to figure out which part of a fight was your fault?

- What are some good ways to make up after you've been mad?

V for Victory!

excluding

- If someone invited your friends to a party and they didn't invite you, how would you feel?

- Would you want to get even and leave that person out of something special?

including

- What can you do to feel better when you are upset about being left out?

- Who could you talk to that might be able to help you?

- Do you always include everyone in your games and parties?

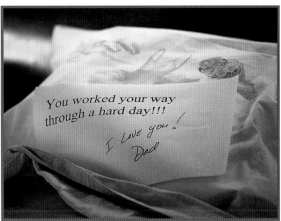

You worked your way through a hard day!!!

I love you!
Dad

Tomorrow is a new day!

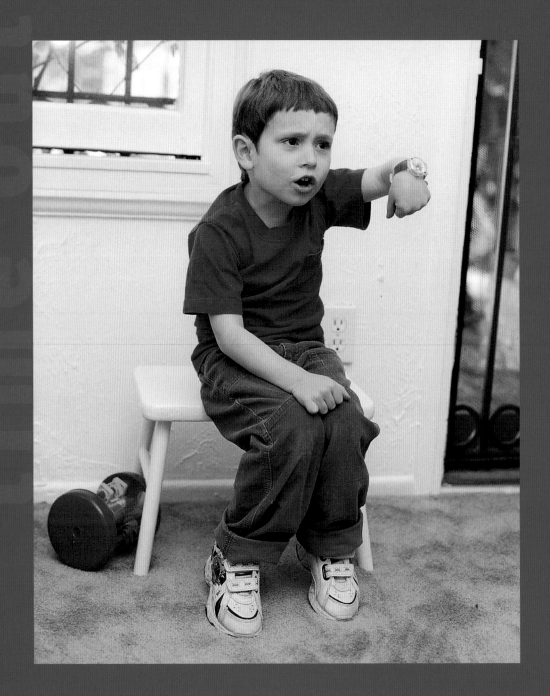

■ Have you ever been in trouble and had to take a time out?

■ Did you keep asking, "Is time out over yet?"

time out

time in

■ What can you do to avoid getting into trouble the next time?

■ Next time you're upset, try taking a "time in" by following these steps:

1. When you feel really upset, sit down and shut your eyes.

2. Take a few deep breaths.

3. Think about solutions to the problem.

4. Let everyone know when you have some ideas that might work.

I'm a problem solver!

■ What would you do if someone in your class whispered something about you that wasn't true?

■ Can you think of some reasons why people lie?

lying

truthfulness

- Who could you count on to believe your side of the story?

- Do you have a friend who could help you talk to the classmate who lied about you?

- Does it feel good to tell the truth?

truthfulness

GENE AND LEE
ARE KIND TO
ALL OF US

JEFF IS A
GREAT
PROBLEM
SOLVER

MARC, MARIA
AND BUTCH
ARE ALWAYS
NICE TO
EVERYONE

We're stars!

poor

poor sport

■ Do you ever play games with someone who is a poor sport?

■ How do they act when they win or lose?

sport

good sport

How do good sports act when they lose?

Is it okay to want to win all the time?

Way to go!

selfishness

- What do you do when someone grabs one of your favorite things?

- If you could have one thing that belongs to a friend, what would you pick?

- How do you think your friend would feel if you just took it?

sharing

- When a friend is coming over, which toys are you happy to share?

- Where could you put things that are just for you?

Good job!

disposable friends

■ Did you ever have a friend who stopped playing with you?

■ Could you figure out why it happened?

■ Have you ever stopped playing with someone? Can you remember why?

friends

dependable

- Describe the kind of friends you like to have.

- Think of five things that make you a good friend.

dependable friends

Thumbs up!

ignoring

- Has anyone ever tickled you even after you yelled, "STOP"?

- What do you say when you think someone isn't listening?

ignoring

respecting

How can you get people to listen to you?

Which grown-ups could help you make others listen when you say, "NO"?

I hear you!

- Do you and your friends ever use swear words? Why?

- Why do grown-ups get so upset when children swear?

swearing

self-control

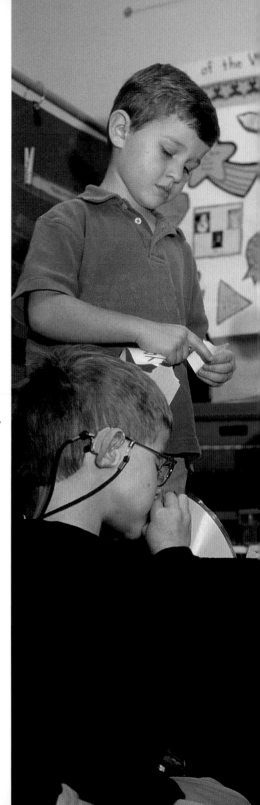

- How do you stop yourself from saying swear words?

- Have you ever thought about writing swear words on paper and throwing them away?

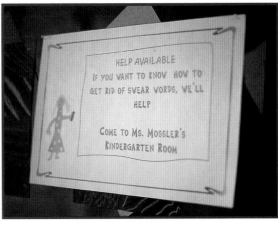

We can help!

55

- How do you feel when someone else gets your parent's attention?

- Why do most children want to feel like their parent's favorite child?

jealousy

acceptance

- Is it okay to feel jealous sometimes?

- How can you make yourself feel better when you feel left out?

A-OK!

acceptance

arguments

arguments

- Have you seen people yelling at each other? How does that make you feel?

- Were you ever in a group when everyone started to argue?

- How do you usually act in the middle of a big argument?

discussions

- If no one was allowed to talk or yell, how would you be able to solve problems?

- Have you ever tried drawing your version of a problem? Do you think everyone who was involved would draw the same thing?

Group hug, everyone!

NOT THE END

What are the three best ideas you found in this book for solving problems?

In your life, what are the hardest and the easiest kinds of problems to solve?

There is a reason why so many of the pages in this book had children and grown-ups congratulating themselves and each other. When problems are solved and over, most people just forget about them. If we celebrate our success, even in little ways, we feel good about what we accomplished.

Do you have other ideas for solving problems and celebrating success? If you send them to me, I'll write back to you. Pretty soon there will be enough ideas for a whole new book.

Remember to take good care of yourself and each other in positive ways!
— Barbara K. Polland

TRICYCLE PRESS • P.O. Box 7123 • Berkeley, California 94707